Carving a Traditional
CAPE COD SIGN

ELDRIDGE

with
Paul White

Text written with and photography by Douglas Congdon-Martin

Schiffer Publishing Ltd

77 Lower Valley Road, Atglen, PA 19310

Dedication

To Barit and Taylor

Acknowledgements

I would like to thank Doug Congdon-Martin for his encouragement, patience, and support during the creation of this book. Thanks also to Cape Forge for supplying the chisels used for carving. I acknowledge all the old timers who have shared their knowledge and the many young whipper-snappers who were wise beyond their years.

Copyright © 1994 by Paul J. White
Library of Congress Catalog Number: 93-87050

Printed in the United States of America.
ISBN: 0-88740-575-4

We are interested in hearing from authors with book ideas on related topics.
DESIGNED BY MARK S. BALBACH

Published by Schiffer Publishing Ltd.
77 Lower Valley Road
Atglen, PA 19310
Please write for a free catalog.
This book may be purchased from the publisher.
Please include $2.95 postage.
Try your bookstore first.

Contents

Introduction:
The Cape Cod Sign Tradition

Rarely is an area associated with a product like Cape Cod is with its signs. The connection goes way back in history, to the time of sailing ships and primitive navigational aids. There were as many as 300 wrecks a year along the Cape Cod shore, and many residents of the area supplemented their livings by salvaging the wrecks.

They would save the people first, and then go back and save whatever else they could, including the ship's figureheads and signs. They saw the beauty in these objects and often used them to decorate their homes.

As transportation improved in the late 1800s, and tourism became one of the mainstays of the Cape's economy, visitors from New York and beyond began to experience the charm of living on the Cape in the summer. Among those charms were the old signs that decorated the homes of the natives. In response to the demand some enterprising Cape Codders sold the old signs as antiques, while others began to carve the signs to order. The earliest recorded request for a carving was in 1928, though it probably started earlier.

Following the Second World War, the mobility of Americans increased and so did tourism on the Cape. More and more people wanted to take home a memento of Cape Cod and a sign was a beautiful and useful token of their stay. That's when carved signs--especially the incised-letter carving--became so popular on Cape Cod. Today there are over 20 commercial sign shops on the Cape, and nearly every one of them offers carved signs. It can be said that there are more sign carvers on Cape Cod than any other comparatively sized place in the world.

The sign in this book is known as a quarterboard. In the days of sailing ships it would have hung on the quarter deck and proudly announced the name of the ship. The shell pattern is an appropriate marine motif, and has been commonly used as an ornament on signs throughout their history. It is finished with paint and gold leaf, which not only gives it a brilliant beauty, but is an enduring finish even when the sign is hung outdoors.

I've explained the process of carving and finishing the sign in a step-by-step fashion. The experienced carver may wish to move quickly through the book, while the novice may wish to have a practice board handy to master the steps before applying them to the finished work.

The main point is to enjoy what you are doing. Every time I read or hear that someone's goal is to retire so they can spend their time in their wood shop, I realize how fortunate I am. I feel as if I retired 27 years ago to my wood shop where I can do what I want, pretty much when I want. It's turned out to be like having a hobby that makes me a good living.

I hope you get as much joy from carving as I have. Good luck!

ABCDEF GHIJKLM

Shell Pattern

NOPQRST UVWXYZ

Carving the
Cape Cod Sign

This sign demonstrates the stages in creating a carved sign.

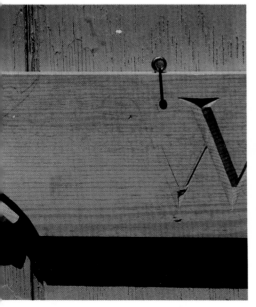

The beginning, of course, is the layout and carving.

Then follows a tinted oil primer. This is thinned by 10-15% with paint thinner. Every coat of paint must be applied with the grain. Next is a white full strength oil-based exterior primer. Then there are three coats of the finish paint. Notice that the letters receive each layer of paint. After powdering the sign, the letters receive the sizing for the gold leaf.

The gold leaf is applied to the letters...

and the decoration for a finished sign.

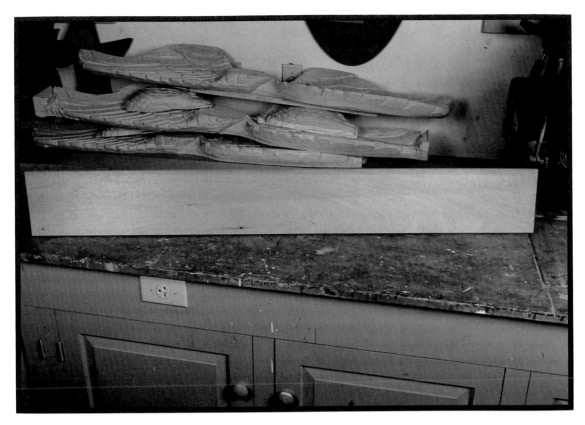

Find a piece of straight grained wood like pine or mahogany. We are using a piece that is 1" x 6" x 48". This piece is mahogany.

Look at the end grain when selecting the piece. It should run as close to vertical to the face of the piece as you can get. As you can see this is more diagonal than vertical, but it should work okay.

Lay the shell pattern at the end of the board.

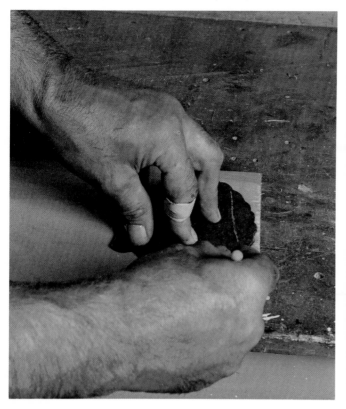

Mark around it.

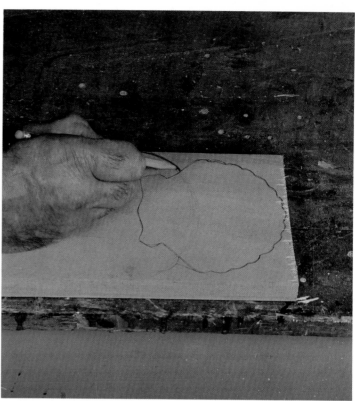

Draw an arc from the edge of the shell to the edge of the board. It may help to use a can or a jar to get a nice arc.

The shell pattern marked. This is a hand-carved sign, so exact measurements are not essential.

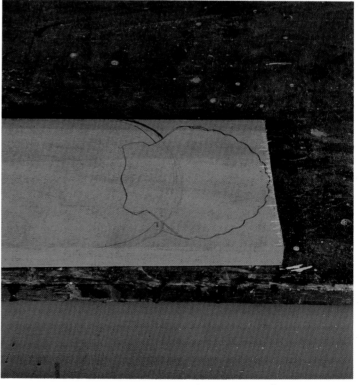

Continue the line through the shell, and draw a matching arc on the other side. Repeat at the other end.

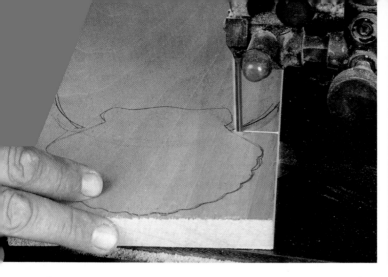

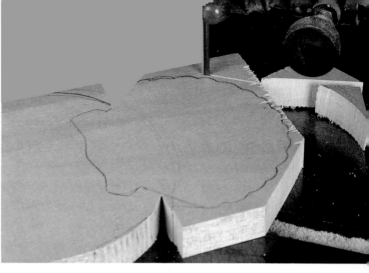

On a bandsaw or with a coping saw cut out the shell pattern. I begin by coming from the side of the board into the V where the shell intersects the arc.

Knock off the corners.

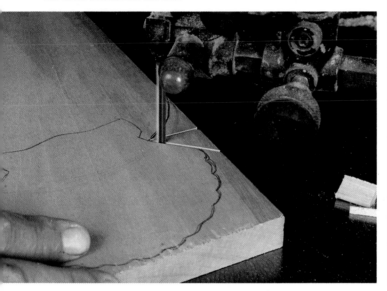

Cut along the edge of the shell to the point...

Cut into each notch of the shell.

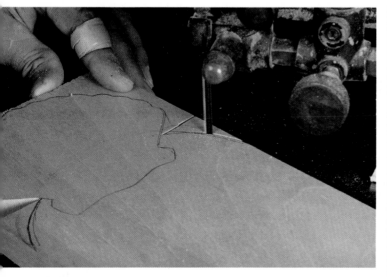

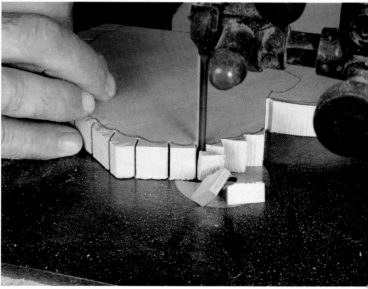

and along arc that defines the shoulder. It is not necessary to do both of these at once. It is more efficient to get one when the board is properly positioned.

Cut back one direction, all around the shell.

This gives you a toothed result.

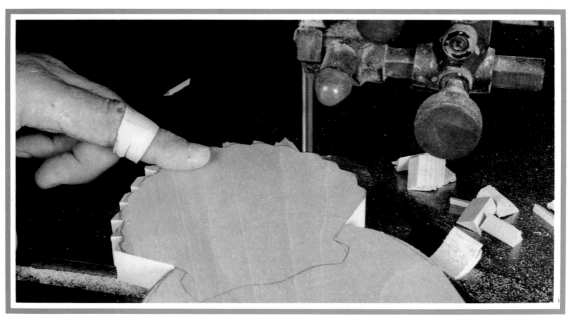

Then cut back in the other direction.

Turn the piece over and clean up spots you couldn't reach.

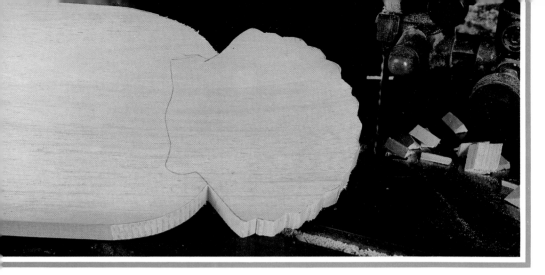

Progress

The layout of letters is more visual than mechanical. They have to look right to the eye. Do your layout work on paper. Start with a center line on the paper, vertical and horizontal. Add a bottom and top line to match the height of the letters. Copy the letters you need at the size for the board, and lay them out on the paper. Adjust them to the proper look.

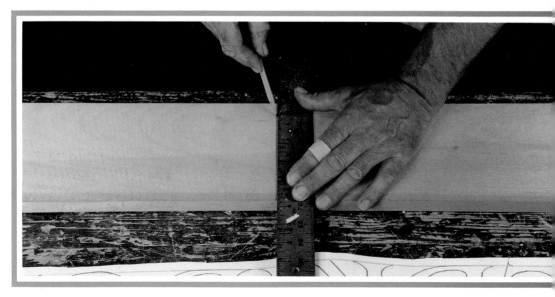

Draw the midline of the board.

A simple way to find the horizontal center to the board is to lay the ruler on a diagonal so its measurement is an even number and mark halfway.

Do the same at the other end...

and connect the dots.

Lay the letter pattern on the board, aligning the midline and center line. Hinge tape in place at the top.

The letters should begin about a shell's length from the base of the shell. If you are using more than one word, the space between words should be considerably less than this.

Lay type writer carbon paper under the pattern.

Run the horizontal line at the top...

and the bottom. This can be a continuous line, because you are going to sand and paint the board.

Copy the vertical and diagonal straight lines, using a rule.

Add the curved lines. Bring the serif to a point for ease of carving.

The result. Before untaping your pattern, make sure you haven't missed any lines. If you have, go back and fix them.

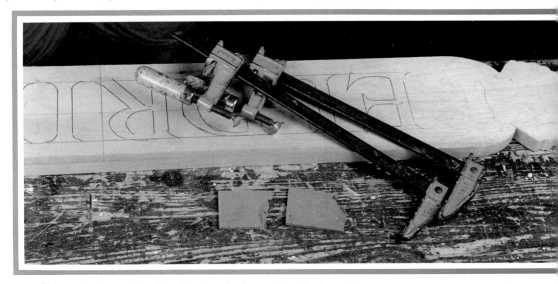

You want to have two hands on the tool, so clamp the board securely to your bench. Pieces of scrap lumber protect the wood from being marred.

Begin the shell carving with a v-tool.

The result

Outline the base of the shell on the outside (board side) of the line. This is a relief cut. The relief cut allows the adjoining slice to be made without tearing.

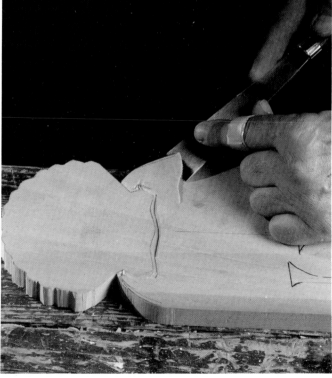

Slice back toward the line from the board. This is a slice, like you would do with bread. You want it to be as smooth as possible. Hold the tool at a 45 degree angle...

and move it across the wood.

Follow the slice again until the wood pops out.

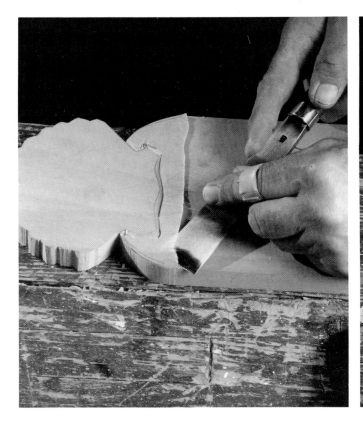

Go all the way across.

Carry this all the way across.

Deepen the line of the shell, using the v-tool. Again, this is to relieve the wood to avoid breakout.

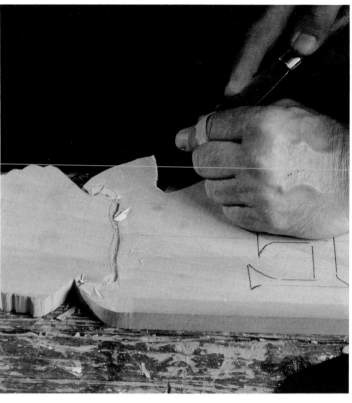

Slice back to the deepened stop.

Try to get the same depth across the piece.

Your goal is to bring the surface of the board down at a nice flat curve. It should not look scooped out or domed. The corners are further along and should be deeper than the center of the board.

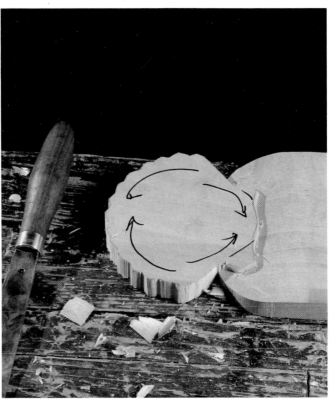

Score the line with a chisel, popping off the shavings.

Wood carves cleanest across the grain, and is okay when doing diagonal cuts. When carving with the grain however, there is a tendency toward ripping and tearing of the wood. For the novice carver, I would suggest drawing the best carving direction on the shell. At the same time draw the line of the ears of the shell.

Clean up the carving.

Follow the line of the ear with the v-tool. This is a relief cut, because it relieves pressure when you cut back to it, preventing chipping.

Think of the shell as a circle with four quadrants. We're going to give it its basic shape with a chisel. Start on the edge of one of the end quadrants and bevel it by slicing with the grain. In a slice the tool is held at a 45º angle to the direction of its movement.

If you go further than this you will being cutting into the grain and things will begin to rip.

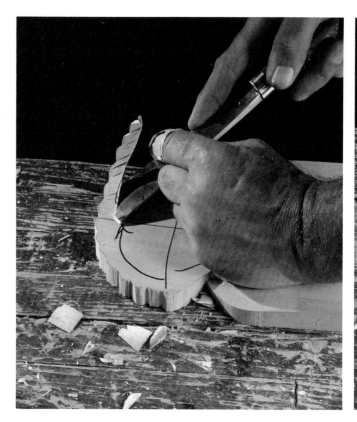

Move across the grain.

Continue in the same way on the next quadrant.

Repeat the process taking away more wood. We will curve the edge of the shell to within an eight or three-sixteenths of the bottom.

Continue to the center where the grain shifts.

You want to keep moving around the piece so it keeps its shape and proportion. You need to rough out the whole shell before you finish any part of it. Move to a back quadrant and start at the side with the same **slicing** motion.

Carve the other back quadrant in the same way.

Slice the ear at an angle, so it slopes down toward the shell.

Deepen the slices on the back quadrants. Remember to keep the tool at a 45º angle to the cut.

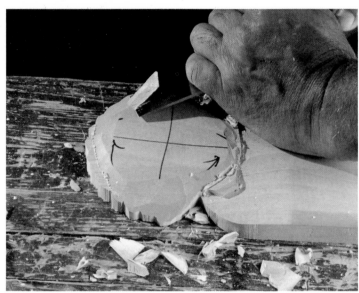

The result.

Go around the shell again...

Deepen the relief cut between the shell and the ear.

establishing the thickness of the shell at the edge.

With the same slicing motion, work from the edge...

Continue on the other quadrants.

back toward the middle, rounding the shell off, still slicing.

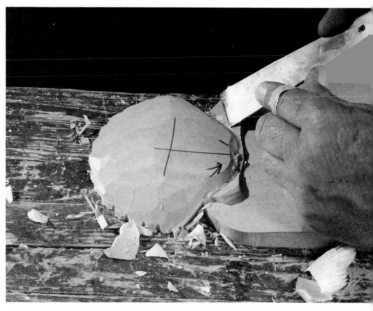

Deepen the ears, keeping the point of the chisel from cutting into the body of the shell.

You will come to some section where you are carving with the grain. This is where the wood will tear and you will have problems. Take light, shallow slices in these areas.

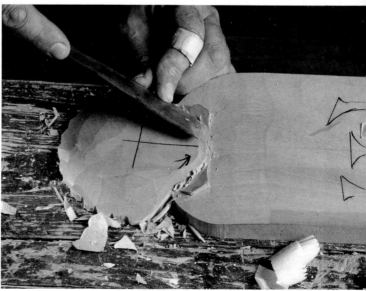

When you clean up the cut, don't cut into the ear.

Rescore the line between the shell and the board.

Start at the heel with a v-tool, and take a very shallow bite toward the outside edge.

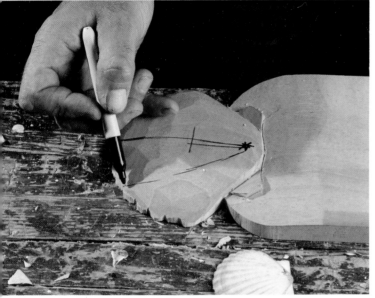

Draw the lines of the rays. These run from the indentations you cut in the outside edge to a center point about a half inch from the bottom of the shell. I usually start at the center, mark a ray about a quarter of the way out, and then fill in the other rays.

Go deeper as you move to the end of the cut. If possible do this in one cut.

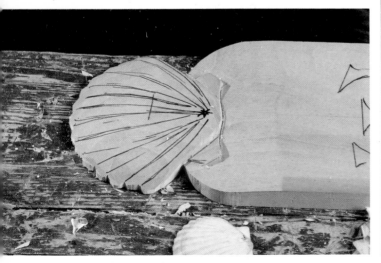

The result.

Continue defining all the rays.

24

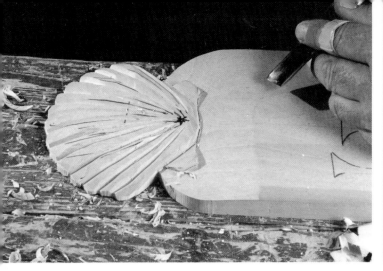

Progress.

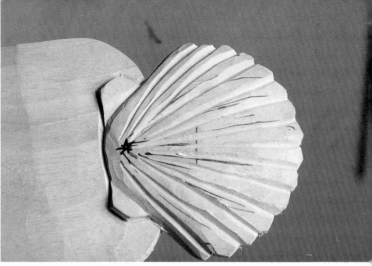

Ready for sanding

Remember we scored the edge of the shell a little while ago. Now we take a small (#3) gouge and undercut it. This involves cutting back from the board along the line of the shell at about a 45 degree angle. The undercutting gives the illusion of far more depth than there is, lifting the shell off the board.

Carve the other shell in the same way.

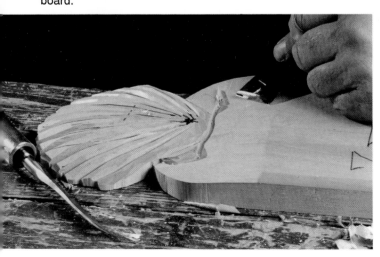

Go back and clean up any imperfections you see.

Begin carving the letters. Normally I would look at the word as a whole and do all the similar strokes working down the word. Like this line of the E...

this line of the L...

this line of the D.

Then I would turn the board around and do another set of similar cuts, like this on the D. You will develop these methods as you are more experienced.

For now let's do one letter at a time. The cuts make a v-cut in each section of the letter. The bevels along each edge are about 25-30 degrees. Envision how it is going to look when it is done. Take a look at the letter plain and try to imagine it finished.

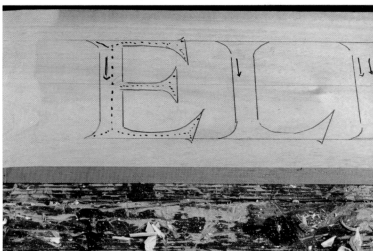

It may help to draw the center lines. Again, take a moment and envision the carved letter.

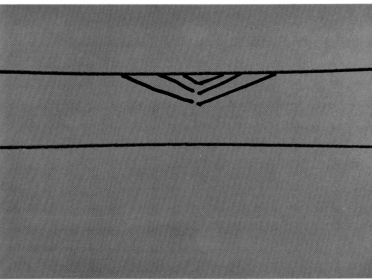

The angle of the cut stays the same, no matter how wide the cut is.

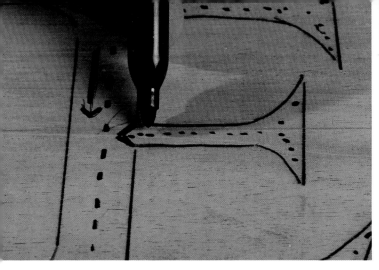

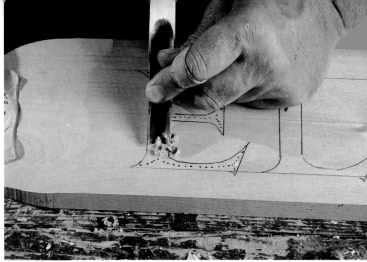

This means that the v-cut of the arm of the E will not come to the center of the vertical element.

Follow the center of the vertical element with a v-tool.

Any letter can be broken down into its component parts. This vertical section of the E is the first one we will relieve.

This gives you a relief cut down the center to avoid breakout.

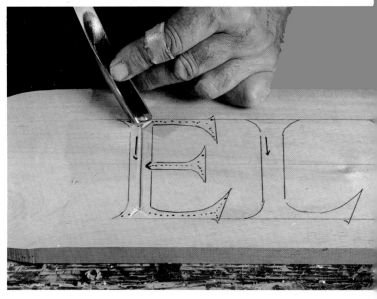

Note that the angles at the ends do not go into the serif of the letter, but into the corner of the vertical piece.

Relieve the angles at the ends. These should start at the edge and go deeper in the middle where they join the center line.

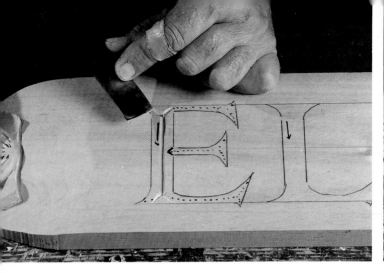

With the chisel at the slope you want for the cut (20-25 degrees), and at about a 45 degree angle to the grain of the wood, start at one of the corners.

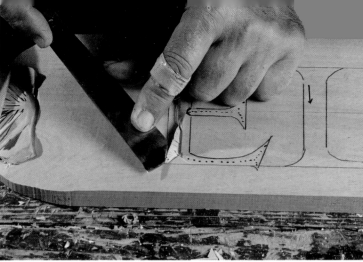

At the end of the stroke, turn the chisel to match the angle at the end.

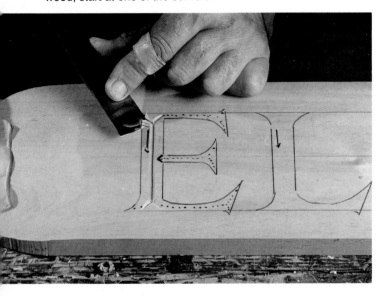

First push the tool straight down without going over the line and cutting into the other side. This gives you a nice clean corner that doesn't need to be gone over again.

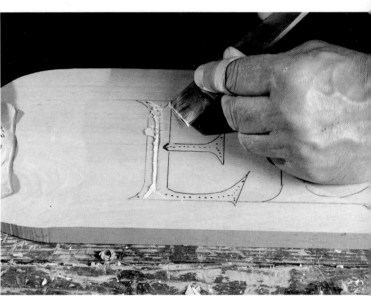

Repeat on the other side. Start at the corner.

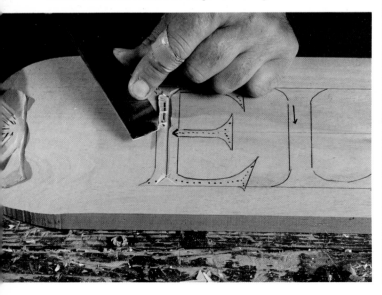

Then move down the letter with a slicing motion.

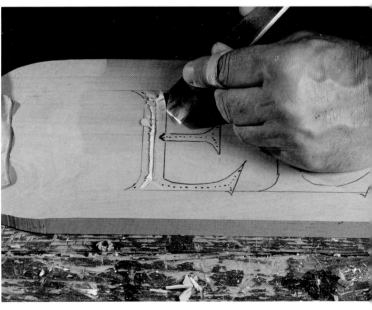

Push in, stopping just shy of the bottom.

Slice down the letter.

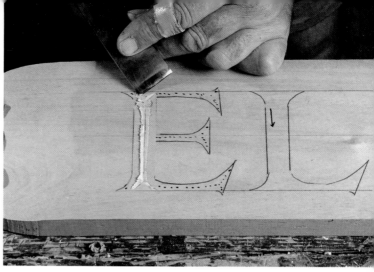

The other cuts go roughly with the grain. To test things don't start right on the line. Instead start a little inside the line and make a slice. This gives you a feel for how the grain is running. In this case it is fine...

Finish the cut as before. Learn to combine the first push with the slice.

so I can go back and start in the corner.

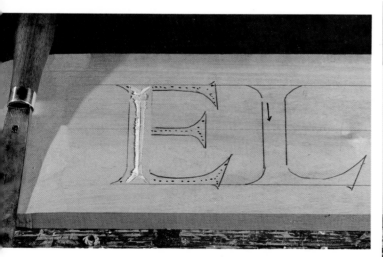

The cut should leave a little wood in the trough. This helps insure against cutting into the opposing plane. This cut has been across the grain, which has given you good control. Wood is a bundle of straws, and cutting the end is more accurate than trying to run your blade down the shafts.

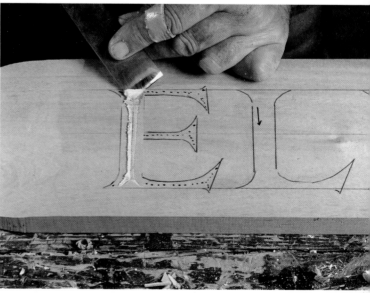

Push down and forward into the trough with a slicing motion.

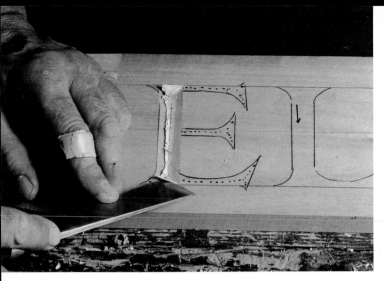

Do the other end the same way.

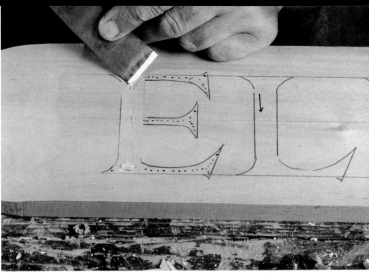

and the ends.

With the point of the chisel go back and clean up the trough. Be careful and try to only go to the bottom of the V.

The result.

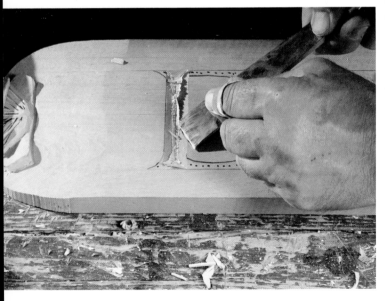

Do the other side...

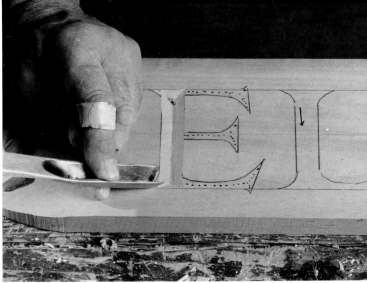

With the v-tool start just inside the corner of the serif and make a relief cut down its middle.

With a straight chisel cut the convex curve, starting at the corner...

Cut relief lines in the center of the arm serifs, starting at the corners and sloping down to the center.

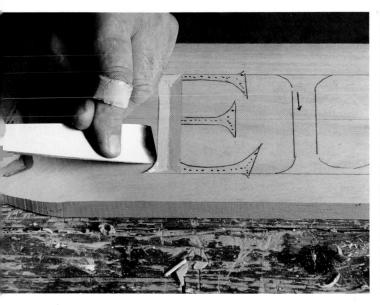

and coming around the curve. With practice you'll be able to come into the straight line in one motion.

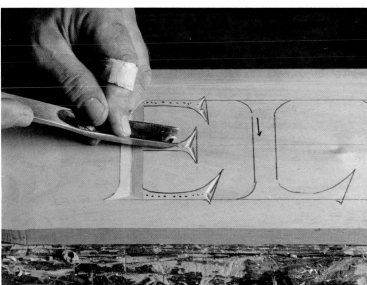

Cut a relief line in the center of the middle arm. The arm is straight, except for the serif, so the line is level and straight.

Slice the straight sides of the serif to match the angles of the ends of the vertical element.

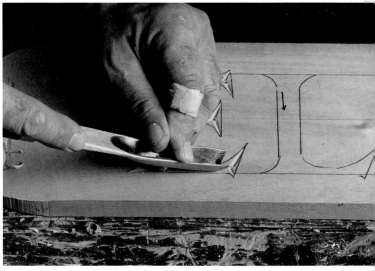

The bottom and top lines get wider at each end, so you need to go deeper as you move out. Start in the middle of the arm...

then work from the center to the vertical member.

Cut the center arm in the same way...

Slice along the plane of the arm.

turning up into the serif. Practice making this in one cut.

At the end turn the chisel into the serif.

If you start here on the bottom arm, you will be going into end grain. Keep thinking about grain as bundles of straw.

Instead start in the middle and slice toward the serif.

ending at the bottom of the trough.

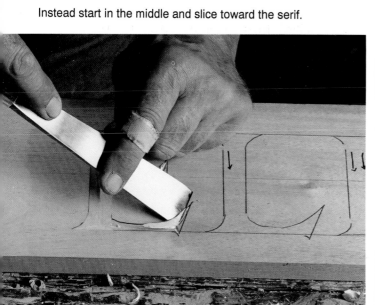

End the cut in line with the center of the serif.

Do the other edges of the arms.

Again, start at middle and cut toward the vertical member...

Again, this cut makes the turn and stops at the angle of the center of the serif.

Slice the ends of the serifs starting at one point and going to the other. Always keep the chisel angle approximately the same, which is 45º to the cut and 25-30º bevel.

When you get comfortable, you can relieve the whole letter at the same time.

The finished E.

Remember, serifs start shallow and go deep.

The top bevel of the letter should all be in the same plane, from serif to serif.

This time we start at the corner with the chisel...

and with one stroke curve around the serif...

and coming down the side.

and come down to the other end. Keep your chisel at the proper angle, both in terms of depth and slicing.

Make a light cut in the end of the serif.

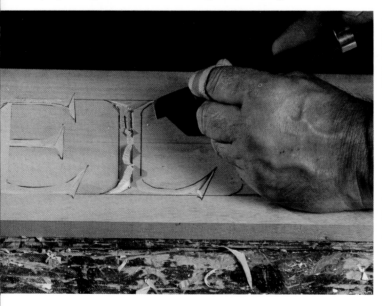

Do the same on the other side, starting in the corner...

Cut the top surface. Since the grain ran favorably in the E, chances are it will here too.

Cut the top edge of the arm, starting at the center and going to the end.

While in this position, finish the top edge of the arm, cutting from the middle to the vertical member.

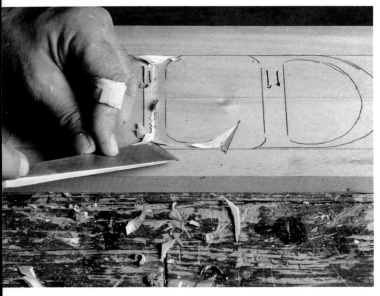

As before I test the grain before cutting the other edge of the L. It runs into the bottom, and will probably rip, so...

Finally cut the little concave portion of the serif. You may wish to switch to a number 3 gouge for this cut.

I come at it from the other side.

Go back over the main vertical element of the letter...

with clean-up slices. Be careful not to let the point cut into the opposite surface.

The relief cut is established.

The D offers a little variation and challenge. The vertical portion is like the other letters with the relief cut down the center and at a constant level. The curve, however is cut from either side toward the middle and gets deeper as the letter gets wider. Start at one end of the curve and cut to the center line.

Start at the corner and cut down the vertical element with one stroke like you did with the L.

Do the same from the other end.

Start at this point to cut the inside curve of the D.

With one stroke, come down to the center line.

Test the grain at the top of the column.

Start about at the same point on the inside bottom curve and come up to the center.

It's o.k. so I slice across the top.

38

Repeat at the bottom of the column.

and the top.

Bring the inside curve back to the center at the bottom ...

Come down the other side of the column.

39

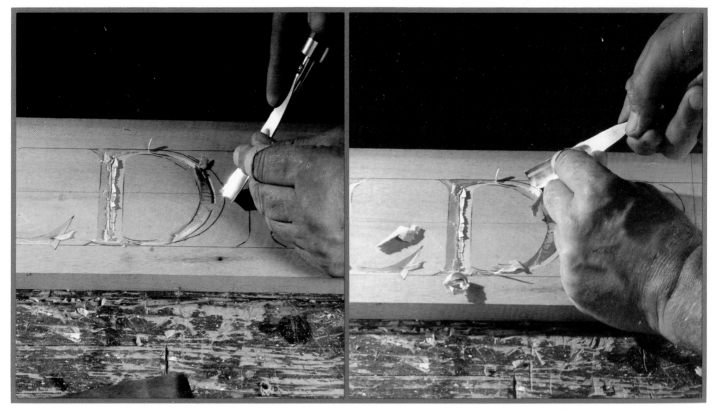

To slice the concave side of the curve, I use a number 3 gouge. Start here and go down the side. This is the first time we have done a concave cut.

Do the same on the top of the curve.

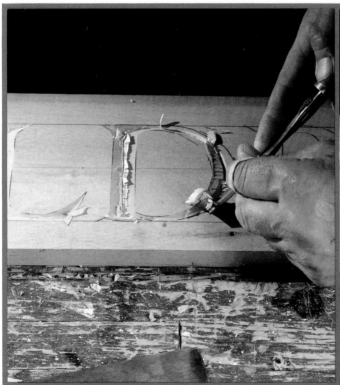

Come around in one cut, keeping the same 25-30º bevel, and keep the tool at a 45º angle to the cut.

Go back and do the clean-up cuts.

The first three letters should give you the basics of carving. You may have had a little trouble making surfaces meet the way you want. This will come with practice. For now, instead of picking and poking, use sandpaper or a rasp. If you don't keep learning the slicing technique, you will not improve.

When you gain confidence you may want to adopt some production methods. I usually make all the relief cuts in in one direction from one carving position.

Then I shift my position and do the relief cuts that are easy from that one.

Continue until all the relief lines are cut.

Then shift position and go the other way. Do as many things as you can in one direction with the tool you have.

Next make all the similar long slices.

Shift to the gouge and do all the concave cuts.

The lettering is finished, and the sign is ready for sanding.

Rasp away any marks left by the bandsaw, particularly here on the corners of the board.

Fold the paper and run it down the ribs of the shell to clean up any tearing that may have occurred during carving.

Use 80 grit sandpaper with the grain to fair the curved portion to the straight.

Go over the surface of the shell. I start out across the grain to remove stock. This will leave sanding marks. Go with the grain to take these sanding marks out.

Use the sandpaper to smooth bandsaw marks and do any necessary reshaping on the edges of the shells.

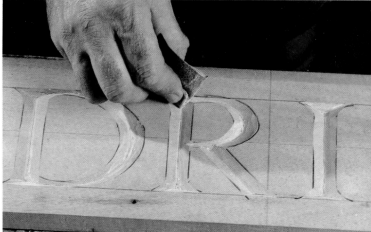

Sand the letters as needed. The main problem area will be at the bottoms of the troughs.

Sand the surface with 80 grit paper to remove milling marks and sharpen the outline of the letter. This can be done with power.

I picked a piece with a flaw so we could talk about repair. This hole beneath the D needs to be filled.

To prepare it, drill into it from two directions with a bit that is about the same size as the flaw. First go one way...

then under cut from another direction.

I use a two-part epoxy auto body filler for repairs. It's hard like clay in 5 minutes so I can carve it, and hardens like a rock in 15 minutes. It is made to go down the highway at 80 mph so it works well for small repairs.

Work it into the hole...

leaving it slightly above the surface. When it dries it will shrink slightly.

Soften the edges of the board. Sharp edges do not want to hold paint. Go over the whole sign with 120 grit sand paper.

Another problem encountered in this sign is a check that showed up in the wood during carving.

If you're proud enough of the work, remember to sign it.

I use a good quality exterior waterproof glue, which I work it into the joint.

When the repairs are dry, sand them over. With the sanding completed you can add hardware. We recommend eye bolts through the top. These should be brass or galvanized.

Painting the Sign

As a primer coat I use a good quality oil-based house primer. I always use paint rather than stain. Stain colors the wood, but does not seal it. When exposed to the weather, stain simply does not protect the sign. These boards with the nails act as stands when we turn the sign over to paint the second side. It rests on the tips of the nails, which create a minimum of marring.

The primer stage is the most important. The first coat is thinned by 10-15% with thinner and tinted a light blue. You can do this by adding a compatible paint or a universal tint. The first coat needs to penetrate and create a bond. The tinting will show through the second coat of white full strength primer at the points you have missed, helping you get complete coverage. All the brush strokes need to go in one direction, with the grain.

Turn it over and start with the recessed areas of the carvings and letters, and pull the paint out. There shouldn't be **any** puddling of paint.

The prime coat raised grain which now needs to be removed. Use 120 grit sandpaper. Preparation is important for good paint and gilding coats. So at this point we need to go over the whole sign. As we did with the painting we will do the deepest parts first. We can see a lot more clearly because of the prime coat.

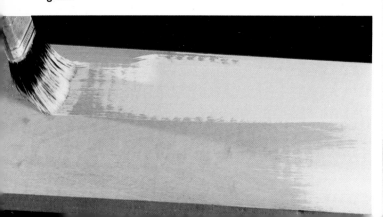

Vacuum or use tack cloth to remove any dust from the piece.

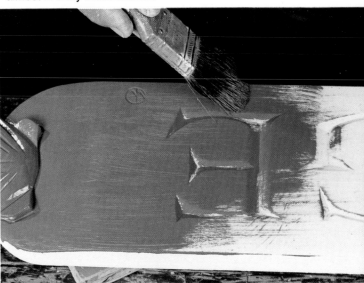

Be sure to go back into the letter and remove any puddles. You can brush this onto the flat surfaces, working it out almost in a dry brush fashion.

For the next coat use a white, full strength exterior oil primer. Start in the recesses of the shell and letters.

After the second coat of primer, check for drips, runs, and dust. Sand only if necessary. Apply the first of three coats of finishing. It should be a good coat, drawn out. It is better to have several thin coats. A low luster exterior oil house paint is my preference. Because the carving always shows better in light colors or gold leaf, it is usually wise to use a dark color for the background. Paint the finish coats over the whole board, even those parts that will be gilded.

Then cover the board.

Let the piece dry over night. Hopefully you have applied a nice thin coat and may not have to sand, but if you do be careful not to sand through to the primer. Apply the second coat of finish paint to the whole piece.

It has had two coats of primer and one coat of finish. Wipe the surface with 220 grit sandpaper if needed.

Flip the piece over. Brush off fingerprints from the underside, and apply paint to the letters first. Follow the shape of the letter...

Go over the surface with a tack cloth to take up all the loose dust.

with the crease of the brush.

Again, begin the final coat on the back. With just enough paint to cover, go with the grain.

Coat the main planes, drawing the paint together with the paint in the letters. Again, remember to paint in one direction.

Go back and feather lightly to remove brush strokes.

Paint the edge last. This allows you to pick up any drips from the face. Pick out any dust, hairs, or flecks while the paint is still wet.

Paint the shell in the same way.

Run your brush along the underside to pick up any drips.

The finished painting.

Gold Leaf

Sizing is done with a varnish-like material called oil size, a product designed particularly for gilding. It provides a smooth, adhesive surface for the gold leaf. It comes in two varieties, the quick dry oil sizing, which we use here, and a long dry sizing, which has the advantage of a larger window of time for applying the gold leaf. This is critical because the most important factor in successful gold leafing is laying it down when the tackiness is just right.

If you put it on when it is too wet it will wrinkle and bleed through and generally look terrible. If it is too dry it will not adhere properly. The tendency is to lay it down when it is too wet. With the quick dry you have a window of about twenty minutes. With the long dry the window is larger, but it takes considerably longer to get to it.

When you purchase gold leaf buy one book of surface gold (loose leaf) containing 25 sheets. It needs to 23 karat gold for use outside. I would recommend you always use this quality. Gold leaf with a lower karat will have more trace metals and will oxidize and tarnish more quickly. A good coat of gold leaf will last 15-20 years. Gold leaf can be found at some art supply houses or from sign suppliers.

and spread it out.

Turn the piece over and apply the powder again...

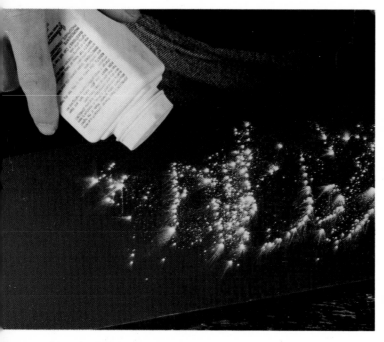

After the final coat has dried it is time for sizing. Cover the whole sign with talcum powder. This will keep the gold from sticking where you don't want it. Powder the back...

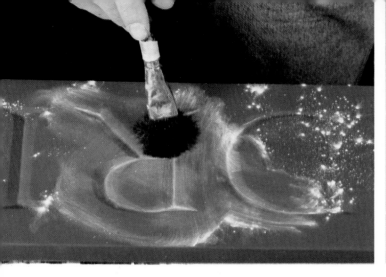

using a brush to get it into the letters.

Thoroughly vacuum the powder off. This removes the excess powder and leaves a fine film. If you don't do this, the sizing will be absorbed by the powder and create problems. The thin film of powder left after a thorough vacuuming will have a minimal absorption effect.

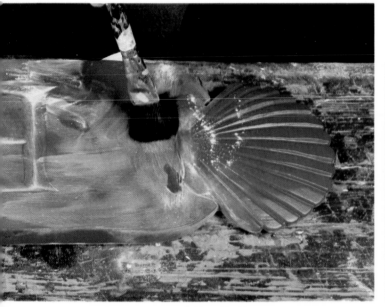

Be sure to get it butted up against the edge of the shell.

Pour a small amount of quick size into a container. You only want to apply sizing to the area you can cover during the window of opportunity. For the beginner I would recommend one or two letters at most. After you get a feel for it you will be better able to judge how much to do at any one time.

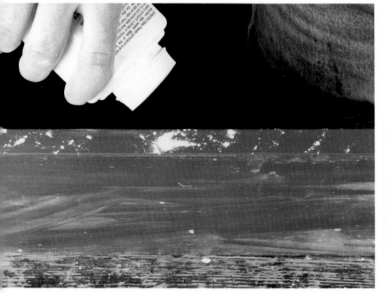

Remember the edge. This is the most likely spot to get some stray gold leaf.

Add a couple drops of yellow tint or a compatible yellow paint. This allows you to see the sizing and to know where it is covering the letter.

Stir thoroughly.

Start with the long straight sides of the letters.

Use the best quality brush for this work. This is a flat gray or brown squirrel hair size 3 quill.

Bring the size to the surface or slightly above. By applying it in nice straight lines, this becomes a chance to clean up the appearance of your carving. Watch for puddling.

Dip the tip of the brush and pull the paint across a palette to pull out the sizing.

Fill in the trough and move to the arms of the letters. Always do the outside first.

The finished E.

Double check the widths. The E was slightly wider than the G. This is easily fixed by adding just a little width with the sizing.

Make sure the width of the vertical element is the same as the widest point of the G for consistency. The sizing step is a time when you can make some adjustments if you have not carved it perfectly.

Start the shell at the close edges. Along the base of the shell, where it meets the board, there should be a space of 1/16" that does not get the sizing or gold leaf. This helps accentuate the shell.

As with the painting, you don't want the sizing pooling in the troughs. Use just enough to cover.

Continue across the bottom, moving as slowly as you can. You want to keep the edge straight and crisp, since this will be the outline of the gold.

Don't forget this corner.

Cover with a nice even coat, following the contours of the shell and getting down into the rays.

When the edge is done move to the creases and the ears.

Be sure to get the edge.

For the main part of the shell you can switch to a larger brush.

When it is covered run your brush through each of the creases to be sure there are no drips.

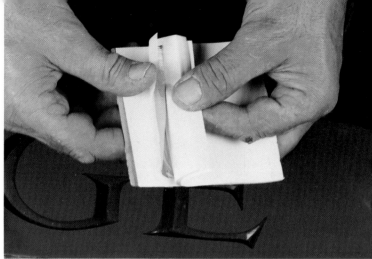

The shell sizing complete. Look at the clock. The fast-drying sizing usually reaches its best tackiness in an hour-and-a-half to an hour-and-three-quarters. This can vary with atmospheric conditions and the brand of size you are using. I keep the palette handy beside the piece so I can see how it is setting by touch. If I touch the carving, it will leave permanent fingerprints.

Carefully open the book from the back, exposing a quarter of a sheet of gold. The gold is very thin and will float out of the book if you are working in a breeze.

When the time has elapsed and the tackiness has become **just barely perceptible** to the touch it is time to apply the gold leaf. Again, this will take some time to get right, and normally you will err on the side of applying the gold leaf too soon, when the sizing is too tacky. I use a super fitch brush, which is a stiff bristled brush, to transfer the gold. Other tools can be used for this. In fact some people use a foam brush.

Back the book of gold leaf with a piece of stiff cardboard.

Most people new to gold leaf plow the brush through the gold leaf bunching it up and making it nearly impossible to apply. I stab the brush at one end of the gold leaf...

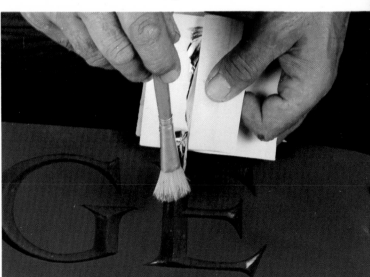

and *lift* it off. This gives me a strip of gold...

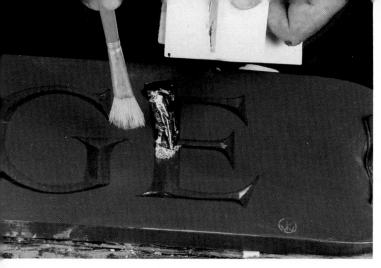

which I lay on the wood. I try to get as big a piece as possible, though there will necessarily be overlapping.

Apply it to the letters.

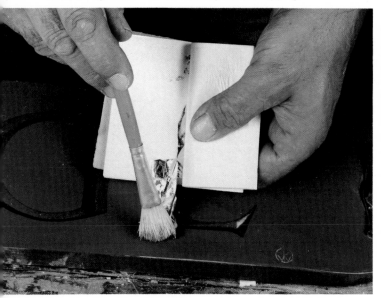

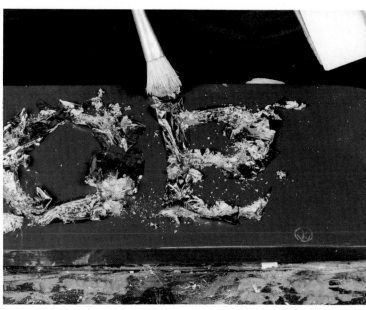

The bottom is done the same way. The thumb holding the book exerts enough pressure to allow a nice clean tear of the leaf.

The gold leaf roughly in place.

Continue to fold the book back to expose more gold.

Gently push the gold into the letter with the brush. Make sure there is gold on the brush and that you don't push bare bristles into the sizing.

56

Continue with the other letter.

You can pull a whole sheet off and let it be pulled on by the sizing.

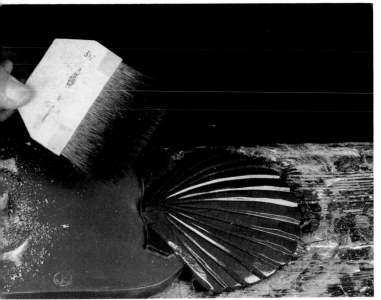

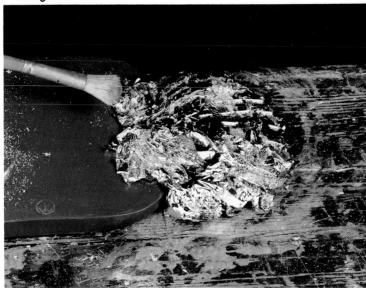

A common tool to do large area like the shell is a gilder's tip. Although it is expensive, it is useful if you are doing a lot of gilding of large areas. For this project we will use another method.

Continue, overlapping for coverage.

Apply the gold leaf to the shell.

Fill in empty spots.

Use the brush to gently push the gold into the carving.

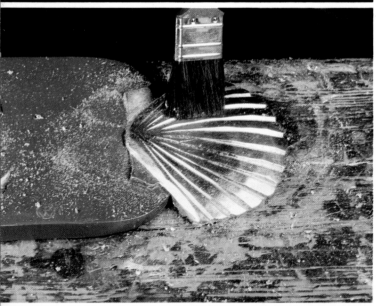

Take a soft bristled brush, such as a water-size brush, and with a circular motion, **lightly** burnish the piece.

Do the same with he letters. Remember to use light pressure. The sizing is not completely dry and you don't want to compress the gold into the size.

Wipe gently with a damp sponge.

A soft cloth will dry it up.

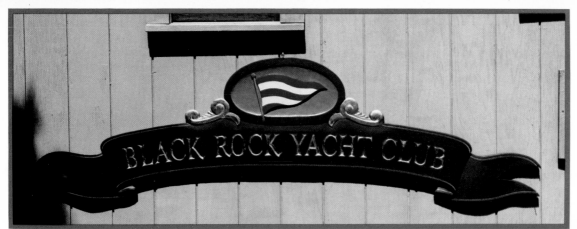